THE KINDNESS Rocks PROJECT™

Thank you for your purchase of The Kindness Rocks Project Kindversations workbook for kids.

Our intention in creating this workbook is to cultivate meaningful conversations with children...our future!

These pages will spark meaningful kindversations in classrooms, in your home, in scouting troops, in therapy practices... anywhere you wish to spark purposeful conversations prompted with pebbles.

We believe that "One message at just the right moment can change someone's entire day, outlook, life!"

Describe a time that you were Brave

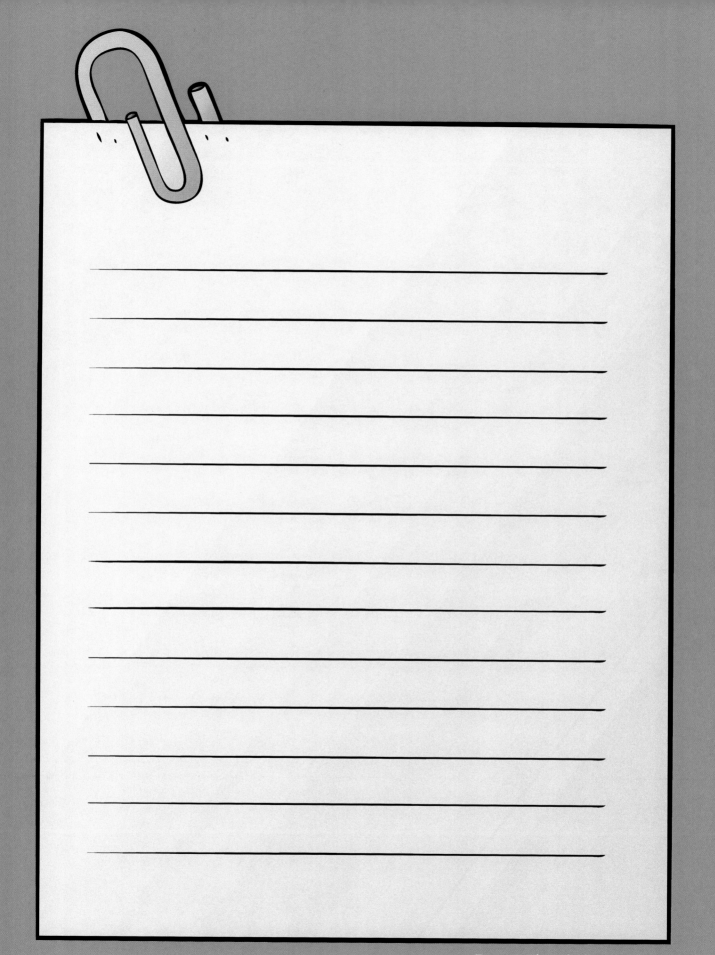

Tell us about a time someone made you feel Special.

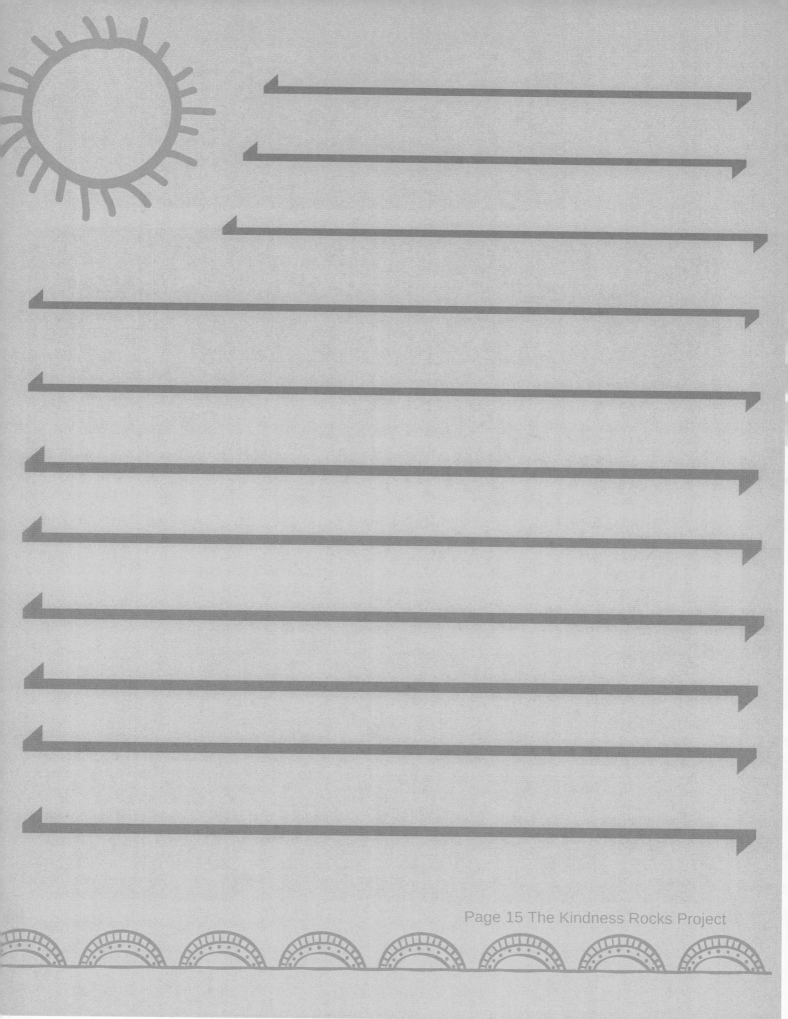

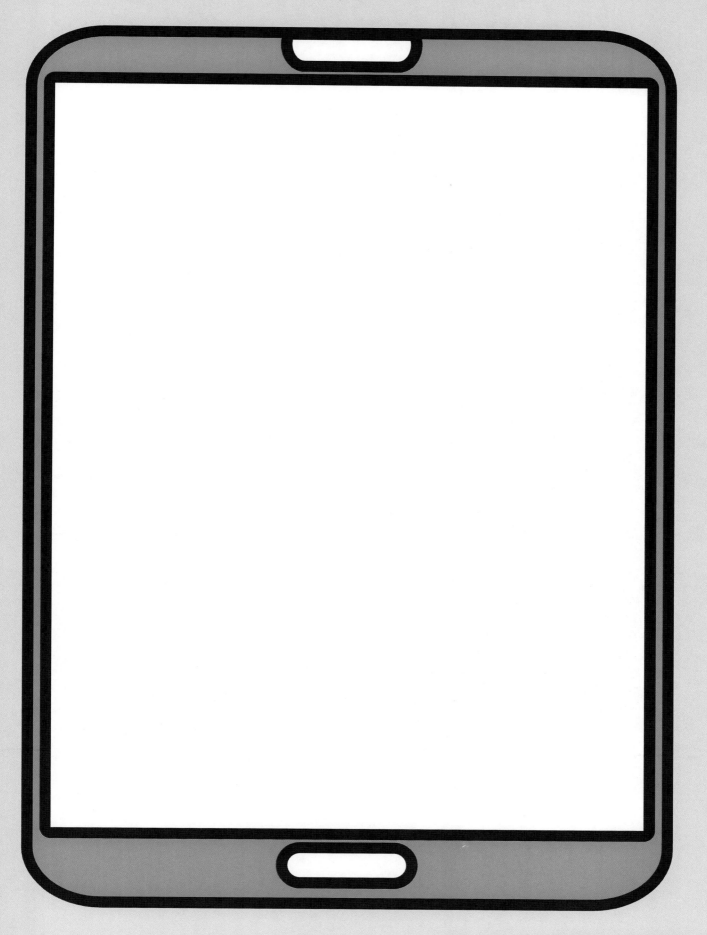

describe
your favorite
piece of clothing
and how it
makes you feel
when you wear it

What are your Favorite things to do over summer vacation?

Create your own Kindness Rock

For more information about
The Kindness Rocks Project & for
other educational curriculum

please visit us at

http://www.thekindnessrocksproject.com

and follow us on social media

Made in the USA
Coppell, TX
22 January 2021